MW00942846

101 Affirmations to Ease Your Grief Journey:

Words of Comfort,
Words of Hope

Harriet Hodgson

BY HARRIET HODGSON

**101 Affirmations to Ease Your Grief Journey:
Words of Comfort, Words of Hope**

By Harriet Hodgson, BS, MA

Cover Design by Jay Highum, Rochester, Minnesota, USA
Photo source www.istockphoto.com

Copyright © 2010 by Harriet W. Hodgson

All rights reserved

ISBN: 1453711880
ISBN-13: 9781453711880

The information in this book is not intended to serve as a replacement for professional advice. Any use of the information in this book is at the reader's discretion. The author and publisher specifically disclaim any and all liability arising directly or indirectly from the use or application of any information contained in this booklet. A medical and/or grief professional should be consulted regarding a specific situation.

101 Affirmations to Ease Your Grief Journey:

Words of Comfort, Words of Hope

By Harriet Hodgson

CONTENTS

PREFACE

Grief is a stressful, scary experience. At a time when you need positives, your life seems to be filled with negatives, and the future looks bleak. How can you change your outlook? You can read affirmations that lift your spirits, illuminate your grief journey, and give you hope.

One affirmation can get you through the day.

This resource contains 101 original affirmations and each is followed by a focus word or words – the root of the affirmation. You may use the focus words for self-evaluation, support group discussions, meditation, or prayer. Like the affirmations themselves, the focus words are timeless. As you continue your grief journey you may return to the affirmations again and again and find new meaning in them.

Though you feel alone now, you are not alone, and this resource is your grief companion. Keep it with you. Tuck it in your purse, briefcase, or backpack. When you are discouraged read an affirmation and think of how it applies to your life. Many affirmations are memorable, but the most memorable may be the last: *My new life is what I make it.*

Reading these affirmations takes little time. Before you head out the door in the morning, read an affirmation to get yourself in a positive mood. You may also copy an affirmation on paper and stick it in your pocket. Though the wording is simple, an affirmation can be complex, far-reaching, and life-changing.

This resource includes the basic affirmation-writing steps. I hope you follow them and write some personal affirmations. I also hope you explore the focus words and see the benefits of self-affirmation. Attitude affects your grief journey and these comforting, hopeful words may be just the boost you need. You can be happy again.

AFFIRMATIONS

1

Grief reconciliation is my responsibility and I accept it gladly.

Focus word: reconciliation.

2

Though I have no control over life events, I have control over my responses to them.

Focus word: control.

3

When the death of my loved one seems like a dream I give myself a reality check.

Focus word: reality.

4

My loved one's values and interests give me the strength to create a new life.

Focus word: interests.

5

I greet each day with a loving and gentle heart.

Focus word: attitude.

6

Grief work takes time and I am taking all the time I need.

Focus words: grief work.

7

Grief will not make me a bad news bear; I will be the bearer of good news.

Focus word: attitude.

8

Joy is joy only when it is shared and I am sharing my new-found joy with others.

Focus world: share.

9

I shall always be a work in progress.

Focus words: personal growth.

10

Hard as it may be, I view each day of my life as a personal miracle.

Focus word: miracle.

11

Life is a search for meaning and, despite my sorrow, I am continuing the search.

Focus word: meaning.

12

Tears are glistening reminders of love.

Focus words: permission to cry.

13

I give myself permission to laugh and am refreshed by it.

Focus word: humor.

14

The bonds of love, when held close, are stronger than death.

Focus word: love.

15

Loss and grief do not make me a bitter person; they make me a better person.

Focus word: determination.

16

This is a day to cherish, for it will not come again.

Focus word: today.

17

No matter what happens, no matter the challenges I face, each day is a spiritual day.

Focus word: spirituality.

18

Writing my grief story is a way to honor my life and loved one.

Focus word: journaling.

19

I treasure the love I shared with my departed loved one(s).

Focus word: love.

20

Changing seasons comfort me and I savor each one.

Focus word: nature.

21

Though I may take unexpected detours, I am still on the recovery path.

Focus word: recovery.

22

I will assess children's sorrow and get help for them if necessary.

Focus word: children.

23

During my grief journey I continue to track my feelings and identify them.

Focus word: feelings.

24

I am the one – the only one – who can define recovery and work towards it.

Focus word: recovery.

25

Down days don't defeat me; they are an opportunity to feel better tomorrow.

Focus word: opportunity.

26

Despite the pain, the one-year anniversary of my loved one's death proves I am a survivor.

Focus word: survivor.

27

Each day I will do something for myself.

Focus word: self-care.

28

If children can live in the moment so can I.

Focus word: moment.

29

I have promises to keep to my deceased loved one, myself, and my life.

Focus word: promises.

30

When I am quiet I tap the wellspring of courage within me.

Focus word: courage.

31

Silence is my introspective friend.

Focus word: introspection.

32

The candle of hope is a fragile, flickering flame and I do all I can to keep it burning.

Focus word: hope.

33

It takes courage to admit I am scared and I credit myself for this courage.

Focus word: fear.

34

In the coming years I will build a new relationship with my deceased loved one.

Focus word: relationship.

35

I am patient with my friends' impatience with my grief.

Focus word: patience.

36

Though death has shaken my world, I am not resigned to it, and continue to take proactive steps.

Focus word: proactive.

37

Hope rises with the sun each morning.

Focus word: hope.

38

My loved one is gone, yet that person is part of my soul.

Focus word: soul.

39

Keeping a routine makes my days and my sorrow easier.

Focus word: routine.

40

As time passes I continue to make good things from grief.

Focus word: good.

41

Staying connected to friends is a continuous goal.

Focus word: friends.

42

Happiness is a personal choice and I choose it for myself.

Focus word: choice.

43

I know the stages of grief are not absolute and often overlap.

Focus words: grief stages.

44

Going backwards on the recovery path does not prevent me from returning to it.

Focus word: regression.

45

Each morning I awaken with a sense of purpose.

Focus word: purpose.

46

Everyone, including me, is worthy of happiness.

Focus word: worthy.

47

During this dark time I am not afraid or embarrassed to ask for help.

Focus word: help.

48

Though everyone responds to grief in similar ways, nobody's grief is like mine, and it is unique.

Focus word: unique.

49

I do not know the future; I only know myself.

Focus word: self-image.

50

Every so often I call time out and take a break from grief.

Focus word: rest.

51

Guilt is a non-productive emotion and I refuse to waste time on it.

Focus word: guilt.

52

Death has lessons to teach me about life and I am learning them.

Focus words: life lessons.

53

Setting new goals is part of my grief work.

Focus word: goals.

54

Giving to others helps me to heal.

Focus word: giving.

55

Though I have lost a loved one, I still have my heritage, education, talents, and soul.

Focus word: self.

56

I claim happiness as mine.

Focus word: entitlement.

57

When people say silly things I ignore their silliness and focus on their caring.

Focus word: caring.

58

Stories about my departed loved one will be told and retold; they will become part of family lore.

Focus words: family stories.

59

Instead of worrying about the future, I focus on today and this moment.

Focus words: living the moment.

60

As I grieve I become more aware of secondary losses and the power of them.

Focus words: secondary losses.

61

Loneliness is not my enemy; it is an opportunity to explore myself.

Focus word: loneliness.

62

Since there are no shortcuts to recovery I avoid them.

Focus word: shortcuts.

63

When I think of sorrow I think of it as a sacred experience and place.

Focus word: sacred.

64

Some friends have drifted away and I am not angry at them for returning to their lives.

Focus word: understanding.

65

My emotional intelligence is a guide that leads me to recovery.

Focus words: emotional intelligence.

66

The kindness of strangers comforts me and I am grateful for it.

Focus word: kindness.

67

Anger is usually part of grief, but not always, thank goodness.

Focus word: anger.

68

If I find myself rushing to avoid grief, I slow down and face my feelings.

Focus word: confront.

69

Death may alter my religious beliefs, yet I can still be a religious/spiritual person.

Focus word: religion.

70

Depression often accompanies grief and if I think I am becoming depressed I will seek medical help.

Focus word: depression.

71

Each day I see where I am on the recovery path and celebrate small victories.

Focus words: small victories.

72

I remember my loved one by preparing his or her favorite foods and enjoying every morsel.

Focus word: memorial.

73

Journaling gives purpose, structure, and clarity to my days.

Focus word: purpose.

74

As I create a new life for myself I draw upon my loved one's strengths.

Focus words: new life.

75

Though I will never get over the loss of my child, I can learn to live with it.

Focus word: acceptance.

76

Personal courage is the ability to trust myself enough to recover from sorrow.

Focus word: trust.

77

As I reconcile my losses I give myself permission to say no to things I do not want to do.

Focus word: no.

78

I say yes to life by learning about grief, laughing more, creating memorials, and setting new goals.

Focus word: yes.

79

To keep grief triggers – anniversaries, holidays, music, and other things – from hindering my recovery I prepare for them.

Focus words: grief triggers.

80

The death of my loved one has shaken my trust in life and I am learning learn to trust it again.

Focus word: trust.

81

When people ask about my departed loved one I thank them for asking and caring.

Focus words: verbalizing loss.

82

Reviewing my relationship with my deceased loved one is part of my recovery plan.

Focus word: relationship.

83

Whether it is writing, singing, dancing, sculpting, quilting, or cheering for life, I express my sorrow in creative ways.

Focus words: creative expression.

84

Though family responses influence me, I have the power to discard a failed "script" and write a new one.

Focus words: family influence.

85

Religion provides comfort, makes me feel good about myself, and the new life I am creating.

Focus word: comfort.

86

Sorrow gives new – and surprising – meaning to my life.

Focus word: meaning.

87

Instead of grieving in isolation I seek social support.

Focus words: social support.

88

Rituals, both old and new, help me to accept loss and move beyond it.

Focus word: rituals.

89

I am creating meaningful memorials in honor of my loved one and benefit from them.

Focus word: memorials.

90

Caring for children, and their faith in me, helps me to heal.

Focus word: healing.

91

Instead of letting pain lead me, I lead the pain.

Focus word: pain.

92

Quiet time is part of each day and in the quiet I am rediscovering myself.

Focus word: quiet.

93

The day will come when I can talk about my loved one without crying and I will celebrate this day.

Focus word: celebrate.

94

When I feel stronger and like myself again I will help others who are grieving.

Focus word: help.

95

I have prepared answers to the awful question, "How are you?"

Focus word: prepare.

96

During my grief journey I continue to redefine my grief work.

Focus words: grief work.

97

Family traditions link me with my loved one.

Focus word: traditions.

98

Each recovery milepost is a reason to celebrate.

Focus word: celebrate.

99

Words are powerful and I let the words I write empower me.

Focus word: writing.

100

With every breath I take I am thankful for the gift of life.

Focus words: gift of life.

101

My new life is what I make it.

Focus words: new life.

AFFIRMATION-WRITING STEPS

These are the basic affirmation-writing steps. Affirmation-writing is a personal process. As you become comfortable with the process you may wish to add sub-steps or new ones. You need a certain mindset to write affirmations and getting that mindset takes lots and lots of practice.

The more affirmations you write, the easier it becomes. Save your affirmations and read them when you feel down. Your affirmations come from experience and may change your life in ways you never dreamed. So put on your thinking cap and get in an affirmation mode. Affirm your life and yourself.

- Begin with quiet, at least 10 minutes, or as long as an hour. Find a comfortable place and clear the clutter from your mind.
- If this is difficult for you, imagine you are looking at stars on a summer night or listening to the soothing sound of waves lapping at the shore line.
- Think of something positive in your life. It can be something small, like a good cup of coffee, or really big like the birth of a child. Life's small things – a smile or laugh – can be powerful.
- Create an affirmation about your positive thought. If you are unable to write a sentence, jot down a word, such as love. Later, you may branch out from this sentence to related words like husband, children, and family support. The affirmation does not have to be in writing; you can remember it.
- Use the present tense. This can be difficult if you have suffered a traumatic loss or multiple losses, but give it a try. Affirm the new life you hope to

create. Your affirmations may start out in the future tense and slowly switch to the present.

- Check your affirmation for tone and word choices. The tone should be positive. Change a word, if you must, but resist the urge to overwork your affirmation and make it longer.
- Stick to one-sentence affirmations because they are easier to remember.
- Write one affirmation per sitting. If other thoughts come into your mind, save them for another time or another day. You may continue to think about them, however.
- Identify the root of your affirmation (called a focus word or words in this book), and write more affirmations about it. Some focus words may startle you and others may lead you in surprising directions.
- Focus words are like arrows and lead you to related thoughts. Follow the direction of your thoughts and write new affirmations. The focus word "routine," for example, may lead to an affirmation about changing your routine. Making a focus word map, with arrows going from the focus word or words to new affirmation ideas, will give you a clearer idea of your thought process.
- Continue to write affirmations. Read them from time to time.
- Look for forward steps in your grief journey.
- Think about keeping an affirmations journal. You may use a notebook, file cards, or computer. Keep the journal for a year, date it, store it in a special place, and begin a new one.

- Apply your affirmations to everyday life. Some grief experts advise mourners to use their affirmations often. Of course this is easier said than done. With practice, however, you will be able to do it. You can live your affirmations and the new life that grows from them.

EIGHT AFFIRMATION-WRITING BENEFITS

Affirmation-writing has significant benefits. As you write your affirmations you are slowly creating a new life for yourself. You are also staying on the recovery path. Here are some benefits of affirmation-writing and you may think of more.

1. **Affirmation-writing is proactive.** Instead of waiting for others to rescue you, you are rescuing yourself. The fact that you are taking a proactive step is empowering and leads to more. According to a *Society for Personality and Social Psychology* article by J. David Creswell and colleagues, self-affirmation can serve as a "buffer to physiological stress responses."

2. **Affirmation-writing requires positive thinking**. Dr. David D. Burns, author of *Feeling Good: The New Mood Therapy*, says moods are created by thoughts. "You feel the way you think," he explains. Though your mind is filled with sad thoughts right now, you can "talk back" to them. You have the mental power to switch from negative thoughts to positive ones. If you are unable to sustain your upbeat mood, at least you have had a mini break from grief.

3. **Affirmation-writing clears clutter from your mind.** You need to be honest with yourself if you are going to accept your loss and move forward in life. Bettyclare Moffatt, author of *Soulwork: Clearing the Mind, Opening the Heart, Replenishing the Spirit*, thinks mental clutter can cloud the joy of life. Her advice: "Go into the attic of your mind and

explore the dusty keepsakes and nightmares that have been stuffed into trunks . . ." Writing affirmations helps you accomplish this mental cleaning.

4. **Affirmation-writing takes less time than a diary or journal.** Diary and journal entries tend to be longer, so they take more time to write. You may think about an affirmation for weeks, but the actual writing – putting words on paper or a computer screen – takes only a moment. This is a definite plus when you are stressed.

5. **Affirmation-writing helps to rid you of pain.** In her book, *Journal to the Self*, Kathleen Adams describes journaling and says you should "allow yourself to feel temporarily uncomfortable." This is okay even if you are making things up. Her point applies to affirmation-writing. Your affirmations may describe an imaginary life and that's okay.

6. **Affirmation-writing moves you forward.** Christina Baldwin, author of *One to One: Self-Understanding Through Journal Writing,* thinks writing about grief teaches us lessons about grief. "We emerge from the grieving process changed people, people who carry the reality of our experience and our grief forward with us into the rest of our lives." This is also true of affirmation-writing; it nudges you along in life.

7. **Affirmation-writing is adaptive.** You can write affirmations any time and any where. Your affirmations don't have to be in writing. Keep some in your mind and recall them when necessary. "We can say our affirmations out loud several times a

day," explains Judy Tatelbaum, author of *The Courage to Grieve.*

8. **Affirmation-writing leads to a new life.** In order to recover from grief you must believe it will end, according to Bob Deits, author of *Life After Loss*. You also have to "be responsible for your own grief process." Deitz continues. Judy Tatelbaum thinks affirmations can become self-fulfilling prophecies. You can explore these prophecies and take action on them. Every affirmation is a brick in the foundation of your new life. Enjoy it!

YOUR PERSONAL AFFIRMATIONS

Write some of your own affirmations here. Be sure to include the focus word(s).

Personal affirmations, continued

MAKE A FOCUS WORD MAP

Write a focus word or words on the left and draw arrows to connecting affirmation ideas on the right.

GRIEF SUPPORT

Street addresses, phone numbers, email and Internet addresses often change. Please check these addresses before you use them. For more support contact local health organizations, hospitals, service agencies, faith communities, and grief counselors. Your public library and church library may also have grief support resources.

American Association of Pastoral Counselors
9504 Lee Highway
Fairfax, VA 22031-2303
Website http://www.aapc.org
Email info@aapc.org

AARP (American Association of Retired Persons) Grief and Loss Programs
601 E Street NW
Washington, DC 20049
Phone 202-434-2260
Toll free 866-797-2277
Website www.griefandloss.org
Email griefandloss@aarp.org

American Cancer Society
1-800-ACS-2345
www.cancer.org, click on Programs & Services

American Hospice Foundation
2120 L Street NW, Suite 200
Washington, DC 20037
Toll free 800-347-1413
Email ahf@americanhospice.org

Association for Death Education and Counseling and
The Thanatology Association
111 Deer Lake Road, Suite 100
Deerfield, IL 60013
Website www.adec.org

American Psychiatric Association
1000 Wilson Blvd, Suite 1825
Arlington, VA 22209
Phone 703-907-7300
Website www.psych.org
Email apaa@psych.org

American Psychological Association
750 First Street NE
Washington, DC 20002-4242
Phone 202-336-5500
Toll free 800-374-2721

Bereaved Parents website, www.Bereavedparentsus.org

Center for Grief Recovery
1263 West Lyola Ave.
Phone 773-274-4600
Email information@griefcounselor.org

Griefs Journey website, www.GriefsJourney.com (primary
focus is the loss of a spouse and life partner)

GriefNet (an on-line support community)
Website www.griefnet.org

Grief Watch website (resources for bereaved families and professional caregivers) www.triefwatch.com

Growth House, Inc. (forum about self-help and recovery)
Website www.growthhouse.org

Mothers Against Drunk Driving (MADD)
511 E. John Carpenter Freeway, Suite 700
Irving, TX 75062
Phone 800-438-6233
Website www.madd.org

National Cancer Institute, 800-4-CANCER, www.cancer.gov

National Self-Help Clearinghouse
1211 Chestnut Street, Suite 1207
Philadelphia, PA 19107
Phone 800-553-4539
Website www.selfhelpweb.org

Open to Hope Foundation (non-profit)
Website www.opentohope.com

The Compassionate Friends (national office)
P.O. Box 3696
Oak Brook, IL 60522-3696
Phone 630-990-0010
Toll free 877-969-0010
Website www.compassionatefriends.org

The Grief Blog (Internet forum supervised by a mother-daughter team of psychiatrists)
Website www.thegriefblog.com

Widowed Persons Service
American Association of Retired Persons (AARP)
601 E Street NW
Washington, DC 20049
Phone 202-434-2260
Toll free 866-797-2277

RESOURCES

Adams, Kathleen, MA. *Journal to the Self: Twenty-Two Paths to Personal Growth*. New York: Warner Books, 1990, p. 105.

Baldwin, Christina. *One to One: Self-Understanding Through Journal Writing*. New York: M. Evans and Company, Ind., 1977, p. 154.

Burns, David D., MD. *Feeling Good: The New Mood Therapy*, original edition. New York: William Morrow and Company, 1980, p. 38, 66.

Creswell, J. David et al. "Does Self-Affirmation, Cognitive Processing, or Discovery of Meaning Explain Cancer-Related Health Benefits of Expressive Writing?" *Society for Personality and Social Psychology*, Inc, March 7, 2007, p. 239.

Deits, Bob. *Life After Loss: A Practical Guide to Renewing Your Life After Experiencing Major Loss*. Cambridge, MA: Lifelong Books (Perseus Books Group) 2004, p.242.

Moffatt, Bettyclare. *Soulwork: Clearing the Mind, Opening the Heart, Replenishing the Spirit*. Berkeley, California: Wildcat Canyon Press, 1994, p. 35.

Rando, Therese A., PhD. *How to Go On Living When Someone You Love Dies*. Lexington, MA: Bantam Books, 1991, p. 254.

Scott, Elizabeth, MS. "How and why to Use Positive Affirmations as a Stress Management Tool," About.com website article

Szpot, Laurie. "The Benefits of Using Affirmations," *Milwaukee Spiritual Journal Examiner*, March 27, 2009 website posting, no page number.

Tatelbaum, Judy. *The Courage to Grieve.* New York: Harper & Row, Publishers, 1980, pp. 100-101.

"The Power of Positive Affirmations," Effective Learning Systems website, no author.

ABOUT THIS BOOK

101 Affirmations to Ease Your Grief Journey came from life experience. On a snowy Friday evening in February of 2007 my elder daughter died from the injuries she received in a car crash. My father-in-law succumbed to pneumonia on Sunday. Two deaths on the same weekend stunned me and I sobbed uncontrollably when I saw their photos on the same page of the newspaper.

Eight weeks later my brother had a heart attack and died. Then in the fall, just when I was starting to come out of the grief fog, my former son-in-law died from the injuries he received in another car crash. His death made my twin grandchildren orphans and my husband and me GRGs – grandparents raising grandchildren. What a journey it has been!

Four deaths in the span of nine months were overwhelming and, since I'm a writer, I decided to write my way through grief. As the months passed my articles became more positive and this led naturally to affirmation-writing, an exercise in positive thinking. I began with an affirmations calendar to go with my current book and also wrote a companion journal with 100 writing affirmations.

Affirmation-writing kept me from wallowing in grief, something I was tempted to do, and helped me cope with multiple losses. One affirmation, "I will get through this," became my mantra and I said it aloud often. I still write affirmations and they appear in my mind unexpectedly. The process is an adaptive one. Writing and reading affirmations keeps me attuned to the miracle of life.

And I have a miraculous new life, a happy life I never expected. This happiness exists because I faced the pain of grief, identified my grief work, and did it. My happiness comes, in great measure, from raising my twin grandchildren. The twins moved in with my husband and me when they were 15 ½ years old. They graduated from high school with honors and are attending college.

I am happy for them and proud to be their grandma.

ABOUT THE AUTHOR

Harriet Hodgson has been an independent journalist for 30+ years. She is a member of the American Society of Journalists and Authors, Association of Health Care Journalists, and Association for Death Education and Counseling (ADEC). Hodgson was a presenter at the 2010 ADEC conference in Kansas City.

All of her writing comes from experience and Hodgson has shared her experiences on more than 160 talk shows, including CBS Radio, and dozens of television stations, including CNN. She has appeared on Healing the Grieving Heart podcasts (www.health.voiceamerica.com) with Drs. Heidi and Gloria Horsley of the Open to Hope Foundation.

The author of 28 books and hundreds of articles about loss and grief, Hodgson is a contributing writer for the Open to Hope Foundation website and an Expert/Platinum Author for www.ezinearticles.com. A popular speaker, Hodgson has given presentations at Alzheimer's, hospice, and health conferences.

Her work is cited in **Something About the Author**, **Who's Who of American Women**, **Who's Who in America**, **World Who's Who of Women**, and **Contemporary Authors**. Hodgson lives in Rochester, Minnesota with her twin grandchildren and husband John. For more information about this busy author and grandmother please visit www.harriethodgson.com.

ALSO BY HARRIET HODGSON

Writing to Recover: The Journey from Loss and Grief to a New Life, Centering Corporation.

This concise grief resource begins with a Foreword by Helen Fitzgerald, Emeritus Training Director of the American Hospice Foundation. It moves on quickly to the Preface, which details the author's experience with multiple losses. Contents include Using This Book, Your Writing Place, Writing Tips for You, Writing and Personal Growth, Readings (30 writing samples), Proactive Steps in This Book, Words of Hope and Grief Support.

Writing to Recover Journal, Centering Corporation.

This companion resource has one purpose – to get you to keep writing about loss and grief. Its 100 writing affirmations foster writing and brighten your days.

Smiling Through Your Tears: Anticipating Grief, Lois Krahn, MD, Co-Author, available from Amazon.

Anticipatory grief is a feeling of loss before a loss or dreaded event occurs. If you're grieving for a sick loved one, a child in danger, a dear friend, or a devoted pet, this book is for you. It is a balm for your wounded soul. The book is filled with Healing Steps – 114 in all – that lead you to your healing path. All of us go through anticipatory grief and, though you can't avoid it, you will survive it.
Along the way you may find yourself smiling through your tears.

24138947R00039

Made in the USA
San Bernardino, CA
13 September 2015